NOVENA TO O(
SORROWS

**A 9-DAY CATHOLIC PRAYER ROUTINE TO
INVOKE OUR LADY'S INTERCESSION IN
TIMES OF SORROW AND SUFFERING**

FR. JEFFERY BEACH

1

Disclaimer

This book is for general informational purposes only and should not be relied upon as religious or spiritual advice. The author disclaims any liability for any loss or damage arising from reliance on information contained in this book. It is not intended to replace professional advice from a qualified religious or spiritual advisor.

Table of Contents

Introduction................................7

How To Use This Novena.....................11

Brief History of Our Lady Of Sorrows...............14

Novena To Our Lady Of Sorrows - Day 1............17

Novena To Our Lady Of Sorrows - Day 2...........19

Novena To Our Lady Of Sorrows - Day 3...........21

Novena To Our Lady Of Sorrows - Day 4...........23

Novena To Our Lady Of Sorrows - Day 5...........25

Novena To Our Lady Of Sorrows - Day 6...........27

Novena To Our Lady Of Sorrows - Day 7...........29

Novena To Our Lady Of Sorrows - Day 8...........31

Novena To Our Lady Of Sorrows - Day 9...........33

Conclusion...........................37

Progress Tracker/checklist...................41

Stay calm and give your desires to God in every situation through prayer and petition, along with thanksgiving. Your minds and hearts will be kept safe by the peace of God, which exceeds all comprehension, in Christ Jesus.

<u>Philippians 4:6–7</u>

Introduction

A weary soul named Emily found herself engulfed by sorrows and tormented by anxiety in the bustling metropolis of Seraphim. She found the pamphlet for the "Novena to Our Lady of Sorrows: A 9- Day Catholic Prayer Routine To Invoke Our Lady's Intercession In Times Of Sorrow And Suffering" while looking for comfort. She made the decision to try it out of curiosity.

With each sincere prayer, a significant transformation got under way. Weeks passed into days, and Emily experienced a sense of calmness. Her worries eventually subsided, and were replaced by a rekindled sense of power and hope. As word of Emily's extraordinary journey circulated rapidly, it encouraged others to find comfort in the Novena. Their burdens were removed, their hearts were repaired, and their faith was recovered.

Are you worn out from bearing the burden of your sadness and suffering? Do you yearn for a heavenly presence to lead you through your life's most trying times? You need look no further as you begin the "Novena to Our Lady of Sorrows: A 9-Day Catholic

Prayer Routine," a profound journey of faith and hope.

You will find a powerful nine-day prayer regimen inside these pages that is intended to invoke the special intercession of Our Lady of Sorrows. This novena is the key to obtaining the consolation and relief you seek throughout your darkest hours.

Who is Our Lady of Sorrows, though, and why does she command such a strong influence over Catholic prayers?

Our Lady of Sorrows has stood out as a symbol of courage and kindness throughout history, resonating with people who needed comfort in their darkest moments. Her story begins with the intense anguish she had while accompanying her adored son, Jesus, as he bore the burden of the world's sins. Our Lady of Sorrows saw the atoning sacrifice that would eternally alter the path of human history from the very foot of the cross.

This unwavering affection and unfailing devotion are what have captured hearts for generations. In order to express their greatest sufferings, ask for her intercession, and find solace in her maternal embrace, Catholics from all over the world have flocked to Our Lady of sufferings. She has evolved into a representation of hope, a means of relieving stress and finding comfort.

This novena is available to everyone who wishes for a special intervention from Our Lady of Sorrows; it is not just for a specific group of people. This prayer regimen provides a haven for people in need, whether you are troubled by emotional turbulence, the weight of group suffering, or personal challenges.

You will be led through thoughtful prayers that have been prepared for you to connect with your own grief each day of this nine-day trip. You will become more intimate with Our Lady of Sorrows as you pray, welcoming her life-changing intercession into yours. As you proceed down this path, you'll learn how resilient you are and how you might be able to find comfort even in the darkest depths of pain.

Beloved, let Our Lady of Sorrows' holy presence fill your heart. Give her permission to walk by your side, to bear your load, and to offer you her tender touch to ease your suffering. Let's go out on this holy journey together, aware that we are not the only ones who suffer.

There is comfort in the arms of Our Lady of Sorrows. There is healing in her kind glance. The secret to gaining access to those blessings lies in this novena. So, let's get started on this nine-day prayer regimen that will change your life, asking Our Lady of Sorrows for a special favor while we look for a way to restore our faith and find peace.

How To Use This Novena

1. **Preparation**: Begin by finding a quiet space where you can dedicate time to prayer each day for the next 9 days. Set aside a specific time that suits your schedule and allows for uninterrupted reflection.

2. **Familiarize Yourself with the Novena**: Read through the entire book to understand the content and structure. Take note of any specific prayers, intentions, or reflections that particularly resonate with you.

3. **Gather the Necessary Materials**: Ensure you have a copy of the book, "Novena to Our Lady Of Sorrows," as well as the accompanying progress tracker in paperback version. The progress tracker is designed to assist you in monitoring your progress throughout the novena.

4. **Day 1**: Begin by opening the book to Day 1 of the novena. Read the introduction and familiarize yourself with the intention for the day. Take your time to absorb the message and reflect on any personal sorrows

or sufferings you wish to bring before Our Lady.

5. **Prayer Routine**: Follow the prayer routine outlined in the book for Day 1. Engage in the suggested prayers, reflections, and any additional prayers that resonate with you personally. The prayers should be heartfelt and sincere, allowing you to communicate with Our Lady and seek her intercession.

6. **Progress Tracking**: After completing the prayers for Day 1, refer to the progress tracker provided in the paperback version. Mark off Day 1 as completed, acknowledging your progress on this fulfilling journey.

7. **Subsequent Days**: Continue this pattern each day for the remaining 8 days of the novena. Follow the guide in the book, dedicating time to reflect, pray, and seek Our Lady's intercession. Allow the prayers to guide your personal reflection, renewal, and healing.

8. **Progress Acknowledgment:** As you complete each day, mark your progress on the progress tracker. This serves as a visual

reminder of your commitment and dedication to the novena, providing motivation and encouragement to continue with steadfastness.

9. Final Day: On the ninth and final day of the novena, celebrate the completion of this spiritual journey. Spend time in heartfelt prayer, expressing gratitude for the intercession of Our Lady and reflecting upon any personal transformation or renewal experienced throughout the novena.

Brief History of Our Lady Of Sorrows

The history of "Our Lady of Sorrows" is a testament to the enduring compassion and profound devotion that Catholics around the world hold for the Blessed Virgin Mary. Also known as "Mater Dolorosa" in Latin, this title reflects the deep sorrow that Mary experienced during her life, particularly as she stood by the foot of the cross during the crucifixion of her beloved son, Jesus Christ.

The roots of this devotion can be traced back to the earliest days of Christianity. Mary's role as the Mother of Jesus made her a central figure in the life of the early Church. However, it wasn't until the Middle Ages that the specific focus on her sorrows began to gain prominence. The seven sorrows of Mary are traditionally depicted as the Prophecy of Simeon, the Flight into Egypt, the Loss of the Child Jesus in the Temple, Mary meeting Jesus on the way to Calvary, the Crucifixion and Death of Jesus, the Descent from the Cross, and the Burial of Jesus.

The devotion to Our Lady of Sorrows has a deep resonance in the hearts of believers. It connects with the human experience of suffering and loss, as

Mary's sorrows symbolize the universal human experience of pain and sorrow. The empathy and consolation that people find in Mary's sorrows mirror their own struggles, reminding them that even in the darkest moments, they are not alone.

The Novena to Our Lady of Sorrows emerged as a profound spiritual practice that spans nine days of prayer and reflection. It's said to have originated in the 13th century with the Servite Order, a religious community founded to honor the Seven Sorrows of Mary. The novena offers believers an opportunity to meditate on each sorrow and seek solace in Mary's compassionate presence.

The impact of the Novena to Our Lady of Sorrows on Catholicism has been profound. It has served as a channel for believers to find solace, strength, and a renewed sense of purpose in their own lives. The novena's structure of daily reflection fosters a deep connection with Mary's experience and allows for personal introspection.

In Catholicism, the devotion to Our Lady of Sorrows is not only a way to honor Mary's role in salvation history, but it also provides a powerful avenue for believers to grow in their faith. By contemplating Mary's sorrows, Catholics are reminded that suffering is not devoid of purpose; it can be transformative and redemptive.

The Novena to Our Lady of Sorrows offers a spiritual journey that resonates with the human soul's longing for comfort and hope. It invites you to draw near to Mary, a mother who knows the depths of suffering and the heights of divine love. Through this devotion, you find consolation, renewal, and the assurance that Mary stands as a compassionate intercessor, ready to accompany them on their journey through life's trials and tribulations.

Novena To Our Lady Of Sorrows - Day 1

In the sanctified names of the Triune God—Father, Son, and Holy Spirit!

Amen.

Introductory Prayer

O grieving Mother, I rely completely on you. You endured the most agonizing pangs of your life as you saw your Son die on the Cross, but you stuck by Him all the way through.

Look kindly upon me, a poor sinner, and get for me from your Son all the graces I require to withstand the afflictions God permits me to go through.

Prayer each day

Her Son was passing away on the Cross.

Mary sobbed as she stood underneath Him, sharing in His redeeming cross.

Her heart is cleaving like a sword as He hangs, and she sobs in sorrow over the terrible loss.

I beg you, O Mother of Sorrows, to make a plea on my behalf before the Sacred Heart of Jesus through your First Sorrow, the prophecy of Holy Simeon *(Explain your dilemma or the specific favor you desire.)*

Concluding Prayer

Memory Rare

Never was it known, O most gracious Virgin Mary, that anybody who ran to your protection, asked for assistance, or sought your intercession was left without assistance. This assurance encourages me to fly to you, O Virgin of Virgins, my Mother. I approach you and stand before you repentant and sinning. O Mother of the Word Incarnate, do not scorn my supplications but rather hear and respond to me in your mercy. Amen.

All hail Mary, you are grace itself.

Please pray for us, Most Sorrowful Virgin.

Novena To Our Lady Of Sorrows - Day 2

In the sanctified names of the Triune God—Father, Son, and Holy Spirit!

Amen.

Introductory Prayer

O grieving Mother, I rely completely on you. You endured the most agonizing pangs of your life as you saw your Son die on the Cross, but you stuck by Him all the way through.

Look kindly upon me, a poor sinner, and get for me from your Son all the graces I require to withstand the afflictions God permits me to go through.

Prayer each day

O the sorrowful, suffering Mother of the Son beyond all others: the only Son of God Most High.

She is heartbroken and her body is shaking as she watches Him as her child passes away.

Intercede on my behalf before the Sacred Heart of Jesus via your Second Sorrow, the Flight into Egypt, O Mother of Sorrows, and obtain for me the favor I humbly beg *(Explain your dilemma or the specific favor you desire.)*

Concluding Prayer

The Memorare

Never was it known, O most gracious Virgin Mary, that anybody who ran to your protection, asked for assistance, or sought your intercession was left without assistance. This assurance encourages me to fly to you, O Virgin of Virgins, my Mother. I approach you and stand before you repentant and sinning. O Mother of the Word Incarnate, do not scorn my supplications but rather hear and respond to me in your mercy. Amen.

All hail Mary, you are grace itself.

Please pray for us, Most Sorrowful Virgin.

Novena To Our Lady Of Sorrows - Day 3

In the sanctified names of the Triune God—Father, Son, and Holy Spirit!

Amen.

Introductory Prayer

O grieving Mother, I rely completely on you. You endured the most agonizing pangs of your life as you saw your Son die on the Cross, but you stuck by Him all the way through.

Look kindly upon me, a poor sinner, and get for me from your Son all the graces I require to withstand the afflictions God permits me to go through.

Prayer each day

Who would not shed tears of empathy if they witnessed Christ's mother sobbing during the painful crucifixion?

Who could not feel her depth of feeling, which revealed the thoughts of many hearts?

Intercede on my behalf before the Sacred Heart of Jesus and grant me the favor I want of you, O Mother of Sorrows, by thy Third Sorrow of the Loss of the Child Jesus. *(Explain your dilemma or the specific favor you desire.)*

Concluding Prayer

Memory Rare

O most gracious Virgin Mary, keep in mind that no one who sought refuge in your care, begged for assistance, or requested your intercession was ever known to have gone unattended. I fly to you, O Virgin of Virgins, my Mother, buoyed by this assurance. I come to you, repentant and heartbroken before you. O Mother of the Word Incarnate, do not scorn my supplications; rather, in your mercy, hear and respond to me. Amen.

All hail Mary, you are grace itself.

Please pray for us, Most Sorrowful Virgin.

Novena To Our Lady Of Sorrows - Day 4

In the sanctified names of the Triune God—Father, Son, and Holy Spirit!

Amen.

Introductory Prayer

O grieving Mother, I rely completely on you. You endured the most agonizing pangs of your life as you saw your Son die on the Cross, but you stuck by Him all the way through.

Look kindly upon me, a poor sinner, and get for me from your Son all the graces I require to withstand the afflictions God permits me to go through.

Prayer each day

She watched Him take the beating while pleading for forgiveness for our misdeeds.

He took on all of our sins.

She was standing there, thinking.

When her Son finally breathed His spirit out in utter despair.

O Mother of Sorrows, through your Fourth Sorrow, as you encounter your Jesus on the road to Calvary, pray to the Sacred Heart of Jesus on my behalf and grant me the favor I beg of you. *(Explain your dilemma or the specific favor you desire.)*

Concluding Prayer

Memory Rare

Never was it known, O most gracious Virgin Mary, that anybody who ran to your protection, asked for assistance, or sought your intercession was left without assistance. This assurance encourages me to fly to you, O Virgin of Virgins, my Mother. I approach you and stand before you repentant and sinning. O Mother of the Word Incarnate, do not scorn my supplications but rather hear and respond to me in your mercy. Amen.

All hail Mary, you are grace itself.

Please pray for us, Most Sorrowful Virgin.

Novena To Our Lady Of Sorrows - Day 5

In the sanctified names of the Triune God—Father, Son, and Holy Spirit!

Amen.

Introductory Prayer

O grieving Mother, I rely completely on you. You endured the most agonizing pangs of your life as you saw your Son die on the Cross, but you stuck by Him all the way through.

Look kindly upon me, a poor sinner, and get for me from your Son all the graces I require to withstand the afflictions God permits me to go through.

Prayer each day

O Blessed Mother, you are the well of love; give me tears to weep for my brother.

Never let my zeal wane.

Let my heart burn freely so that Christ, my God, will be happy to see me completely consumed by love for Him.

Standing at the foot of your dying Son on Mount Calvary, O Mother of Sorrows, in your fifth sorrow, please ask the Sacred Heart of Jesus to intercede on my behalf and grant me the favor I want. *(Explain your dilemma or the specific favor you desire.)*

Concluding Prayer

Memory Rare

Never was it known, O most gracious Virgin Mary, that anybody who ran to your protection, asked for assistance, or sought your intercession was left without assistance. This assurance encourages me to fly to you, O Virgin of Virgins, my Mother. I approach you and stand before you repentant and sinning. O Mother of the Word Incarnate, do not scorn my supplications but rather hear and respond to me in your mercy. Amen.

All hail Mary, you are grace itself.

Please pray for us, Most Sorrowful Virgin.

Novena To Our Lady Of Sorrows - Day 6

In the sanctified names of the Triune God—Father, Son, and Holy Spirit!

Amen.

Introductory Prayer

O grieving Mother, I rely completely on you. You endured the most agonizing pangs of your life as you saw your Son die on the Cross, but you stuck by Him all the way through.

Look kindly upon me, a poor sinner, and get for me from your Son all the graces I require to withstand the afflictions God permits me to go through.

Prayer each day

I beseech you, O Holy Mary, to embed His wounds firmly inside my heart so that I can carry them as well.

I want to take on the weight that He was carrying and share in His sorrow.

O Mother of Sorrows, may the Sacred Heart of Jesus intercede on my behalf and grant me the favor I beg of you. Through thy Sixth Sorrow, thy Jesus is laid in thine Arms. *(Explain your dilemma or the specific favor you desire.)*

Concluding Prayer

Memory Rare

Never was it known, O most gracious Virgin Mary, that anybody who ran to your protection, asked for assistance, or sought your intercession was left without assistance. This assurance encourages me to fly to you, O Virgin of Virgins, my Mother. I approach you and stand before you repentant and sinning. O Mother of the Word Incarnate, do not scorn my supplications but rather hear and respond to me in your mercy. Amen.

All hail Mary, you are grace itself.

Please pray for us, Most Sorrowful Virgin.

Novena To Our Lady Of Sorrows - Day 7

In the sanctified names of the Triune God—Father, Son, and Holy Spirit!

Amen.

Introductory Prayer

O grieving Mother, I rely completely on you. You endured the most agonizing pangs of your life as you saw your Son die on the Cross, but you stuck by Him all the way through.

Look kindly upon me, a poor sinner, and get for me from your Son all the graces I require to withstand the afflictions God permits me to go through.

Prayer each day

Let me join you in your mourning and shed unceasing tears for Jesus' Crucified throughout my life.

Let me stand by your side as you cry, maintaining vigil on death's behalf the entire day.

O Mother of Sorrows, may the Sacred Heart of Jesus plead on my behalf and grant me the favor I want of Him via your Seventh Sorrow, the Burial of your Son. *(Explain your dilemma or the specific favor you desire.)*

Concluding Prayer

Memory Rare

Never was it known, O most gracious Virgin Mary, that anybody who ran to your protection, asked for assistance, or sought your intercession was left without assistance. This assurance encourages me to fly to you, O Virgin of Virgins, my Mother. I approach you and stand before you repentant and sinning. O Mother of the Word Incarnate, do not scorn my supplications but rather hear and respond to me in your mercy. Amen.

All hail Mary, you are grace itself.

Please pray for us, Most Sorrowful Virgin.

Novena To Our Lady Of Sorrows - Day 8

In the sanctified names of the Triune God—Father, Son, and Holy Spirit!

Amen.

Introductory Prayer

O grieving Mother, I rely completely on you. You endured the most agonizing pangs of your life as you saw your Son die on the Cross, but you stuck by Him all the way through.

Look kindly upon me, a poor sinner, and get for me from your Son all the graces I require to withstand the afflictions God permits me to go through.

Prayer each day

Queen of the virgin choir, please do not criticize me when I strive to imitate your sincere tears.

Let me honor Christ's wounds and share in His suffering as He died a painful crucifixion.

We thank God for exalting His holy Cross and beg the Mother of Sorrows to intercede on our behalf. *(Explain your dilemma or the specific favor you desire.)*

Concluding Prayer

Memory Rare

Never was it known, O most gracious Virgin Mary, that anybody who ran to your protection, asked for assistance, or sought your intercession was left without assistance. This assurance encourages me to fly to you, O Virgin of Virgins, my Mother. I approach you and stand before you repentant and sinning. O Mother of the Word Incarnate, do not scorn my supplications but rather hear and respond to me in your mercy. Amen.

All hail Mary, you are grace itself.

Please pray for us, Most Sorrowful Virgin.

Novena To Our Lady Of Sorrows - Day 9

In the sanctified names of the Triune God—Father, Son, and Holy Spirit!

Amen.

Introductory Prayer

O grieving Mother, I rely completely on you. You endured the most agonizing pangs of your life as you saw your Son die on the Cross, but you stuck by Him all the way through.

Look kindly upon me, a poor sinner, and get for me from your Son all the graces I require to withstand the afflictions God permits me to go through.

Prayer each day

Intoxicated with love for Him who endured, let me experience the suffering He offered.

May I absorb His wounds as mine own.

May my heart be ignited and flaming on the day of Christ's coming.

Help me at His throne, virgin.

May His Cross act as a bridge and my victory cry be His death.

May He keep me in the grace of God.

May my soul awaken in splendor when my body is stolen by death and take up residence in heaven. Amen.

On this final day of our novena to you, Blessed Mother, we entrust ourselves to your heart, which is punctured with love for your Divine Son. *(Explain your dilemma or the specific favor you desire.)*

Concluding Prayer

Memory Rare

Never was it known, O most gracious Virgin Mary, that anybody who ran to your protection, asked for assistance, or sought your intercession was left without assistance. This assurance encourages me to fly to you, O Virgin of Virgins, my Mother. I approach you and stand before you repentant and sinning. O Mother of the Word Incarnate, do not scorn my supplications but rather hear and respond to me in your mercy. Amen.

All hail Mary, you are grace itself.

Please pray for us, Most Sorrowful Virgin.

Conclusion

As you reach the conclusion of this transformative journey through the "Novena to Our Lady of Sorrows," pause for a moment and reflect on the profound impact this prayer routine has had on your heart and soul. Over the course of these nine days, you have diligently sought the intercession of Our Lady of Sorrows, imploring her to alleviate your burdens and offer solace in times of sorrow and suffering.

Throughout the rich history of Catholic prayers and Christendom, Our Lady of Sorrows has held a special place in the hearts of believers. Her unwavering strength and unwavering love have provided comfort to countless individuals who have faced their own trials and tribulations. She stands as a beacon of hope, an advocate for those in need, and a motherly figure who understands the depths of our pain.

Through this novena, you have entered into a sacred dialogue with Our Lady of Sorrows, pouring out your emotions, fears, and sorrows before her. You have witnessed the transformative power of prayer, as the weight of your burdens has been slowly lifted from your weary shoulders. In every moment of devotion, you have grown closer to her, fostering a deep connection that will continue to resonate within you.

Remember the testimonies shared at the beginning of this booklet, where brothers and sisters like you found solace, relief, and answers through the intercession of Our Lady of Sorrows. Their stories are a testament to the miracles that await those who wholeheartedly embark on this prayer routine. Let their experiences ignite your faith and fuel your resolve to seek Our Lady's intercession.

Within the pages of this book, you discover prayers that resonate with your desires and struggles. You experienced the power of intentional and fervent prayer, trusting that as you surrender your intentions to God, He will respond in His divine wisdom and love.

Remember, brethren, that this novena is not a mere recitation of words but a genuine conversation with the divine. It is an opportunity to draw closer to God, to seek His guidance, and to find solace in His presence. As you diligently engage in these nine days of prayer, allow yourself to be vulnerable and open to the transformation that awaits you.

Now, as you come to the end of this novena, it is not a farewell, but rather an invitation to integrate the lessons learned and the strength gained into your daily life. Carry the devotion, faith, and healing experienced during these nine days with you, allowing it to guide you through future challenges. Our Lady of Sorrows is ever-present, ready to hear your prayers and provide comfort in moments of despair.

Embrace the power of this novena, for it is not limited to a select few. It is a sacred offering for every seeker, for every individual who yearns for a special intervention from Our Lady of Sorrows. She knows the depths of your heart and the intricacies of your sorrows. Open yourself to the possibilities that lie ahead, knowing that you are not alone in your journey.

In closing, remember that your journey does not end here. It continues with every prayer, every moment of reflection, and every act of faith. May the Novena to Our Lady of Sorrows serve as a catalyst for positive change, healing, and transformation in your life.

Beloved, let the flame of devotion burn bright within you. Embrace this special prayer routine as a lifelong companion and continue to witness the miracles of Our Lady of Sorrows in your own life. Step forward with renewed faith, knowing that you are forever connected to her loving presence. Seek her intercession, trust in her compassionate embrace, and experience the boundless grace that awaits those who believe.

To enhance your novena experience, the paperback version of this book offers a progress tracker. This valuable tool allows you to mark each day of prayer, creating a visual representation of your journey towards reflection and renewal. By using this tracker, you can witness the growth and transformation that takes place within you throughout the nine days.

Take the first step now. Begin your novena, and with every prayer, draw closer to the loving embrace of Our Lady of Sorrows. In moments of sorrow and suffering, find comfort in her intercession, knowing that she hears your cries. Trust in her, place your sorrows at her feet, and open yourself to the transformative power of her love. The miracles are waiting.

Progress Tracker/checklist

Days	Prayers	Reflections
1		
2		
3		
4		
5		
6		
7		

8		
9		

Instructions :

1. Each day, mark the corresponding checkbox to track your progress through the novena.
2. Alongside each day, you can add any personal prayers.

Note: By using this progress tracker, you can easily keep track of your journey through the 9-day novena to Our Lady of Sorrows providing a visual representation of your accomplishments and prayer reflections.